Craig Stadler's
SECRETS OF THE SHORT GAME

Craig Stadler's SECRETS OF THE SHORT GAME

Craig Stadler

with Dawson Taylor

CONTEMPORARY
BOOKS, INC.
CHICAGO ▪ NEW YORK

Photos by Jeff McBride and Joaquin Bengochea

Copyright © 1987 by Craig Stadler with Dawson Taylor
All rights reserved
Published by Contemporary Books, Inc.
180 North Michigan Avenue, Chicago, Illinois 60601
Manufactured in the United States of America
Library of Congress Catalog Card Number: 87-13539
International Standard Book Number: 0-8092-4945-6

Published simultaneously in Canada by Beaverbooks, Ltd.
195 Allstate Parkway, Valleywood Business Park
Markham, Ontario L3R 4T8 Canada

To Sue
Craig Stadler

To Denny, Christine, Dawson,
and their charming mother,
Mary Ellen
Dawson Taylor

CONTENTS

We would like to express our appreciation to the PGA National Golf Club and to Atlantis Golf Club for their permission to photograph this book on their fine courses.

Thanks, too, to our excellent models and good golfers themselves: Julie Kintz, Mary Last, and Jim Patty.

Craig Stadler's
SECRETS OF THE SHORT GAME

HOW THIS BOOK CAME TO BE WRITTEN

The day was Wednesday, April 7, 1974, and I was about to indulge myself in my favorite pastime—following the newest stars of the international golf circuit in their practice rounds at Augusta National Golf Club as they prepared for the 38th Masters tournament.

There are no announced pairings on that day. The golfers make up their own foursomes, the "names" with other names, and the unknowns with other unknowns. I walked up the fairway to the first green. It is quite a long and arduous walk uphill, but the view is spectacular from behind the green as the golfers' shots come arching onto the velvet surface. I watched a pair of golfers play the hole and then saw the man I recognized as Craig Stadler. He had hit a tremendous drive only a wedge distance away from the green. His second shot nearly holed. I decided to follow him and his partners around the course.

The program told me that he had qualified for the Masters by reason of the fact that he had won the United States Amateur Championship the previous year. Robert T. "Bobby" Jones always believed in inviting the leading amateurs to his tournament and so every year the semifinalists of the Amateur are extended an invitation to play in that prestigious tournament. Most often those amateurs are seldom heard from afterward

1

but they do have their moments of glory playing with Arnie or Jack or Lee.

That day I saw Craig Stadler exhibit a most remarkable touch around the greens and on the closely cut, even icy, slopes of the greens. Craig did not win that first Masters. Rarely does a newcomer win that tournament. It takes a great deal of experience to fathom the intricacies of the Augusta National course.

During the next few years, I followed the career of Craig Stadler, adopting him as my imaginary horse in the professional golfers' race to glory and tremendous sums of money. When Craig broke through to win the 1982 Masters I was right there in the gallery cheering him on. I agonized with him when he apparently blew his chances to win by losing strokes to Dan Pohl on the back nine and was lucky, in my opinion, to back into a tie with Pohl. I followed the playoff down the 10th fairway certain that Pohl had the momentum and would win the title. But Craig must have summoned all his talent and ability for that one hole, as he played it perfectly and won with an easy par 4 to Pohl's disastrous 5. I was delighted. My man had won.

So you can imagine my surprise and delight when my editor suggested that I help Craig Stadler write a book on his magnificent short game. Craig happened to be playing in the Disney World tournament at that time. I live in Florida now so it was easy for me to arrange to meet Craig at Orlando. We agreed that a book by him on the short game might be a valuable contribution to the library of golf and decided to proceed with the project.

About a month later, Jeff Mc Bride, official photographer of the PGA, photographed Craig in many different short-game shots and situations.

From that point the book began to take shape. There were two sets of photographs—one for Craig, one for me. We numbered them in sequence so that when Craig, out in California, was looking at photo 24, for example, I was looking at the same photo.

We spent many hours discussing and analyzing the physical and the mental aspects of the short game. When you read the chapter on awkward shots you should be aware of the fact that as Craig was standing in the grass of one of the bunkers he was attacked and bitten by a nest of fire ants. This truly was bravery above and beyond the call of duty.

As for my own credentials in golf and writing, I have been an avid follower of the golf scene since the 1937 United States Open at Oakland Hills, which was my home course at that time. I have written a number of books on golf history and the golf swing. I helped Horton Smith write his book *The Secret of Holing Putts*. I also worked with Gary Wiren on *Super-Power Golf* and on his new book, *Sure Shot*. I have played to a low handicap all my life. It is presently a 4. I hold two course records—one at the Detroit Golf Club and one at Atlantis Golf Club.

Craig and I both hope that the combination of his knowledge of the golf swing and my ability to put it down in writing has resulted in a book on the short game that will be of great help to golfers everywhere.

INTRODUCTION

I was born in San Diego, California. My father was an avid golfer—not an especially good one, but one who loved the game. When I was only five I tagged along with him and played golf with shortened clubs.

Later on we lived outside San Diego near a deep canyon. I can remember using an old iron club and knocking stones high in the air over the canyon and watching them fall to the bottom.

Golf is an unusually individual game, the golfer alone against the golf course. Most other games pit one opponent against another, teams of players against other teams of players. Even in tennis where matches are head to head the conduct and play of one player greatly affects the play of the other.

Unlike many other sports one can play golf all alone and enjoy the competition of self against par, the prescribed number of strokes that a good golfer should score in driving his ball from a designated teeing area a few hundred yards down a fairway so as to roll it into a small hole in an area of closely cut grass called a green.

I have always loved to play golf. I used to play nearly every day on a public course that required every kind of golf shot. The greens there were very fast, so at an early age I learned how to putt on extremely difficult greens.

5

I began to play tournament golf when I was in my early teens. Along the way I won the World Junior Championship, the San Diego City Amateur Championship, and the Southern California Interscholastic.

When it came time for me to go to college I really wanted to go to the University of Southern California. The coach there was the famous Stan Wood, who had developed some great golfers and golf teams. Oddly enough, I happened to win an amateur tournament that Stan was observing. It was a great coincidence for me because the result was an offer of a scholarship at USC.

I played golf on the college golf team and did well. I remember one time when I threw a club in anger. Coach Wood called me into his office and told me that the next time I threw one I would no longer be a member of the team. I never threw one again—that is, one that he could see.

In my junior year of college I went to the U.S. Amateur Championship which was played at the famous Donald Ross course at Inverness near Toledo, Ohio. I was fortunate enough to win, and I began to consider making my career as a professional golfer.

However, I decided to stay in college for my senior year and get my degree in business administration first. This turned out to be a wise decision. I was pleased to be selected as one of the members of the Walker Cup Team in 1975 which was victorious over a strong British-Irish team at St. Andrews, Scotland.

I became a professional golfer in 1975 and, I am sorry to say, at first I definitely did not set the tour on fire. It took me seven years to accomplish the task, but in 1982 I became the number one money-winner on the tour with $446,000 in earnings. I won four tournaments that year, one of my best.

Now I'd like to tell you a little bit about my credentials for writing this book on the short game. When I was young I devoted as much as four hours a day practicing all the shots around the green and putting. I would practice in the late afternoon until it got so dark I couldn't see the ball.

The result of all that practice was that I learned how to get "up and down"—get the ball within three feet of the hole most of the time and sink the putt.

Last year I led the PGA Tour as the best putter with an average of 29.63 putts per round. From a statistical standpoint that means I averaged 6.37 one-putt greens per round. I was also the leader in breaking par 21.8 percent of the time.

These facts and statistics attest to my skill around the greens and on the putting surfaces. I assure you that I do know a great many secrets of the short game. In this book I hope that I can convey all of them clearly and simply for you to understand and follow.

Craig Stadler

1
THE PITCH SHOT

The Pitch Shot—a shot of varying length in which the ball is lobbed or lofted in the air. It is often not a full shot, usually one of 100 yards or less.

The Encyclopedia of Golf

The game of golf would lose a great deal of its lure and pleasure if there were no creeks, bunkers, hills, and hazards on the courses of today. So, successfully meeting and conquering a formidable hazard is an important part of a good golf game. Frequently you will find yourself in a situation that requires you to loft the ball out of its lie into the air and over some hazard or other obstruction that prevents you from getting to the hole in a more direct fashion. Most often the problem will be a yawning bunker between you and the green. Or it might be anything from a small pine tree to a huge spreading oak tree.

The shot required is called a pitch shot. It is played with one of the more lofted irons, the 7-iron, 8-iron, 9-iron, pitching wedge, or sand wedge. Your own judgment of the trajectory of the shot required will determine the club you will use to accomplish your objective. If your ball is 60 to 70 yards from the green and the obstruction or hazard is not so high that it forces the selection of a more lofted club you may prefer to use your 7-iron or 8-iron. If your ball must get up into the air quickly and also stop quickly on the green once it gets there your choice may be your pitching wedge or even your sand wedge.

The most important thought to keep in mind is the primary purpose of the shot—to get the ball up and over the bunker or obstruction that faces you. In general, I advise you to use more club than you might think is necessary for this type of shot.

To illustrate what I call the principle of "more club than necessary," let's consider a trouble situation and see how it applies. Let's say that you are confronted with a fair lie in the rough and your ball is approximately 80 yards from the green. There is a small pine tree 15 feet high twenty yards ahead and it lies directly in your target line. Furthermore, there is a deep bunker in the front face of the green. It is also directly in your line to the flagstick. Let's say, for example, that with a fairway lie, no pine tree, and no yawning trap—just a clear open green to approach—you would usually use an 8-iron for the shot.

The presence of the hazards brings the "more club than necessary" theory into operation. You definitely do not want your ball to fall short and into the bunker. You really do not know until you hit the ball how much more power you might need because of the additional resistance of the wiry grass in the rough. Another factor here, a psychological one, comes into play.

When you know you have sufficient power in your club, that you have a club strong enough to make the shot, you are more relaxed about your situation and will swing more freely. More often than not you will be successful in the shot, carrying over the tree and the bunker.

The same "more club than necessary" principle also applies to a shot where you must loft the ball over a tall tree on your way to the green. I will agree that if it is possible it is better to go around trees or under their branches than over them in most situations. But every golfer, sooner or later, is confronted with a situation in which he must have his ball carry over a tree or trees on its way to the green.

Let us presume that your first appraisal of the lofted shot over the tree leads you to a decision that a 7-iron would supply sufficient loft to do the job. Your lie is good, the ball is sitting up well, and you expect to get the club on the ball fairly so that the club loft will work efficiently. The "more club than necessary" theory is that you should take an extra number—an 8-iron, with even more loft than the 7-iron—and thus be certain that you have enough loft to carry the tree. In this case the "more club" rule means that you take a club with greater loft.

The "more club than necessary" theory is an excellent one to keep in mind not only when you execute trouble shots but also on many other occasions such as when you have wind in your face or are playing in cold weather, which lessens the resiliency of the golf ball and thus the power of a given club.

Robert T. "Bobby" Jones was famous for taking more club than he really needed for a particular shot. He preferred to execute a smooth, easy swing rather than force any club to give him extra distance. Jones played that way and was so successful he became one of the best players in the world. I think it is wise for us to imitate his style and thinking. I do on many occasions and recommend the "more club than necessary" theory to you.

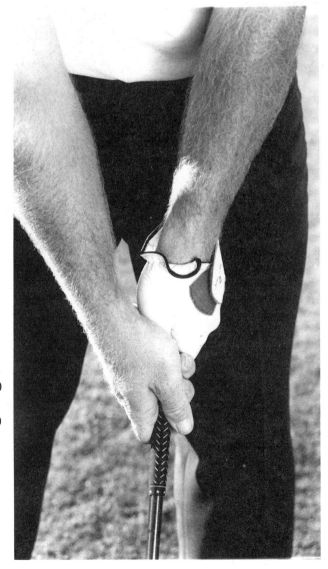

Here is a view of my grip for a full shot with a pitching wedge or sand wedge. I would call it a moderately strong grip; the "V" of my right thumb and forefinger points toward my right shoulder and the "V" of my left thumb and forefinger points to my chin.

Here is a view of my grip and stance for a full sand wedge shot. They would be the same for a pitching wedge shot. Notice that the ball is played slightly back in my stance, more toward the center. This ball position allows a more descending blow upon the ball and results in more backspin on the shot.

A side view of my stance for a full wedge shot. Notice that my head, my hands, and the club shaft are all in a straight line to the ball. My stance is square to my intended target line. A line through my shoulders would point to my target.

The first foot of my takeaway for the full wedge shot. There is no wrist movement so far. My left shoulder initiates the swing while my arms, hands, and left knee all begin to move in one synchronized motion. My weight is primarily on my left side and will stay there throughout the swing.

My wrists remain unbroken for the first foot or so of my backswing. I try to make everything move at once in what is called a one-piece takeaway— my left shoulder, my arms, my hands, my left knee. My head remains fixed and steady in order to give me a central point about which the swing revolves.

My takeaway for the wedge shot. I break my wrists quickly as I come away from the ball. Then I keep them broken until late in the downswing when I release them through the ball.

The same wedge shot with my swing at the shoulder mark. Notice my steady head, my full shoulder turn. I am thinking "slow, easy, don't hurry."

The top of the backswing on a full wedge shot. I keep my weight on my left side throughout the swing while I make a full shoulder turn. The ball is played off the inside of my left foot. My swing is a three-quarter one for better control.

A head-on view of a full shot with the sand wedge. This shot I am going to "knock down" by playing the ball back toward the middle of my stance. From this position I can strike down on the back of the ball and impart backspin which will cause it to stop quickly on the green.

The follow-through on a cut sidespin full wedge shot. Because of the outside-in swing which puts the cut spin on the ball, the follow-through is lower and more around the body than it is on a normal full shot.

Here is a view of my setup for a 50-yard pitch with my sand wedge. Notice that the ball is played back more toward the middle of my stance. That is so that I can strike a more descending blow than usual. It helps to put backspin on the ball and stop it quickly on the green. The white line shows my squareness to the line of intended flight. A line through my shoulders and my knees would run straight at the flagstick. To shorten my distance I have gone down on the shaft nearly to the bottom. This adjustment in grip gives me my standard 50-yard shot.

Here is another view of the 50-yard pitch shot with a sand wedge. This time I am going to aim the ball to the left of the flagstick with some left-to-right sidespin and let it kick to the right. Notice that I have opened my stance slightly by drawing my left foot away from the line. My weight is entirely on my left side and will stay there throughout the swing.

Here is the start of the backswing of the 50-yard pitch shot in the preceding photo. Notice how quickly I have broken my wrists as I come away from the ball. The swing will not be very long, only to shoulder height. My head remains extremely steady, unmoving, as I turn my shoulders away under my chin. The slightest head movement can be devastating because it will result in a mis-hit shot.

I am at the top of my backswing on this 50-yard pitch. My weight has remained on my left side although my shoulder turn is full. I am looking intently at the back center of the ball and will keep my eyes there until I have struck it. I find this is a good way to insure that I stay down on the shot and do not come off the ball at impact.

The follow-through on the 50-yard pitch shot is full and unhurried. There is a pleasant rhythm to a 50-yard pitch. Since it is far less than full strength I am able to make an easy swing, letting my clubhead do the work. I control my distance by gripping the club shaft down low and by limiting my backswing to shoulder height.

The final resolution of the pitch shot swing, the thrill of golf. The ball has landed about ten feet to the left of the hole and, with the sidespin I imparted to it, has rolled to the right close to the hole.

Here is my stance for a normal pitch shot in the 35-to-40-yard range. Notice that my stance is slightly wider than it was in the following shot of the 25-yard wedge shot. I can control the distance of my wedges by going down on the shaft and by shortening my swing. I try to make every swing, whether full or less than full, with the same easy rhythm and a full follow-through.

Here is my stance for a 25-yard pitch with my sand wedge. Notice that I have narrowed my stance and shortened my grip almost to the steel shaft. The ball is played off a line running outward from the inside of my left shoe. My hands and the club shaft are on a straight line to the ball. This would be a standard pitch shot with normal run and no effort on my part to put extra spin on the ball.

When you have a short lofted approach to a green well protected by a front bunker and a flagstick cut close to the front of the green, it is very useful to put a backspin on the ball to cause it to "bite" and stop quickly on the green.

There are several conditions necessary for the shot, the main one being a clean hit so that no grass will get between the ball and the face of the club. Secondly, you must play the ball off your left heel and open the clubface slightly at address. You are going to cut the ball with a clean stroke that will put spin on it. The more steeply you come down on the back of the ball the more spin you will get. So start the swing by picking the club straight up from the ball. It won't really be straight up, but it will be picked up earlier and straighter than in the normal swing.

Once you have reached the top of your backswing you must really turn on the power in your downswing. I have the feeling that I am driving the ball down into the turf. The loft of the club does the work of putting the ball into the air and the downward blow on the back of the ball causes it to rotate backward with a spin that continues until it strikes the surface of the green and "bites" or spins backward. Don't let your hands roll over at impact or you will not get the effect you want. Your hands should move straight out toward the hole and only long after the ball has been sent on its way will you finish your forward swing and allow your hands to roll over.

A view of a sand wedge pitch shot over a hazard to a closely cut hole. Notice that I have opened my stance by drawing my left foot away from the target line. I take my club away from the ball on the outside. When it returns to the ball it imparts a cutting action. The ball will rise quickly because of the opened blade and sit down on the green quickly because of the cut or sidespin on the ball.

A view of the sidespin cut shot with the sand wedge near the top of the backswing. In this swing the hands do not go back any farther than waist high. The quick action of the hands and wrists delivering the descending blow on the ball plus the substantial weight of the clubhead itself help me to make the shot almost effortlessly. I try to be slow, relaxed, and rhythmic with my swing and let the club do the work.

Another view of the sidespin cut shot with the sand wedge. The outside path of the club can be clearly seen. My wrists have broken quickly. My hands will return the club to the ball with a sharp descending blow from the outside and put a left-to-right spin on the ball. I will aim this shot a few feet to the left of the flagstick to allow for the kick to the right.

Here is an interesting and difficult pitch out of easy rough to a flagstick closely cut on a downslope near the edge of the green. The margin of error is very slight on a shot like this. The ball must land in the fringe of the green on a spot no larger than one foot in diameter. If it lands beyond that spot it will run by the cup a considerable distance. I have opened the face of my sand wedge and play the ball well forward in my stance. I can "see" the ball in its higher trajectory traveling up nearly straight into the air and then I visualize it landing softly on the fringe and trickling down to the cup.

Here is the backswing on the shot in the preceding photo. My hands go no farther than waist high. My wrists are broken quickly in my backswing. I am very leisurely with this swing, almost lazy. I let the clubhead do the work of sliding under the ball and popping it up into the air. My head is very still and unmoving. My body movement is minimal, too.

Here is the finish of the high soft pitch in the preceding two photos. Notice that I have made a full follow-through with a high finish with my wedge. Although the ball is well on its way my body has remained steady, unmoving. The complete finish is most important on a shot like this. I have the feeling that because of my leisurely swing the clubhead is more in control of the shot and will do the job if I just allow it to go through the ball properly.

A sand wedge pitch shot from moderately deep greenside rough. This is a difficult shot for any golfer because taking too much or too little grass before striking the ball will ruin the shot. The sand wedge is the safest and most effective. Play the shot the way you would a bunker shot of similar distance with the ball lying cleanly. Pick out a spot in the grass a couple of inches behind the ball. Concentrate on letting your club go through that spot with a full follow-through. Use more power than you think you should—most shots of this type fall short of the hole.

Here is a real "bird's nest" lie in deep rough. Use your sand wedge and concentrate on hitting the grass behind the ball, counting on the force and loft of the club to do the work. A full follow-through is important.

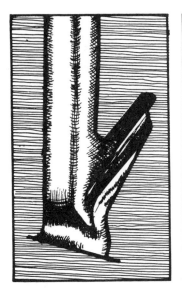  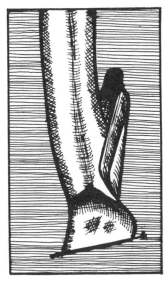

Wedges are manufactured these days with different overall weights and with soles that "bounce" or "dig" depending upon the angle of the sole as it strikes the turf. This drawing illustrates these characteristics. The wedge on the left would bounce, while the one on the right would dig into the sand or ground.

2
CHIP-AND-RUN SHOT

*Chip—a short approach consisting almost
entirely of run. It is usually played from just off
the green with a variety of clubs.*
                              The Encyclopedia of Golf

The chip-and-run shot is executed with any club from a 4-iron down through the 8-iron. Over time you will develop a favorite club for this shot. For the average player this is most frequently the 5-iron, probably because it gives a nice medium trajectory to the shot—not too high, not too low.

When do you use the chip-and-run shot? The first requisite is that you do not have to contend with a bunker or severe undulation in the surface of the green. It is meant to be used when the distance is just a few yards too long to putt. The idea is to chip the ball over rough terrain or the fringe of a green that would interfere with the accuracy of a putt that must roll all the way to the hole.

The general rule of thumb for this shot is to plan a one-third chip and two-thirds run to the flagstick. That is, plan to loft the ball the first third of the distance and let it run the other two-thirds of the way to the cup. Since your overall distance will vary from shot to shot it is clear that you must be flexible in your club selections. One time you may use your 5-iron, another time your 6, and so on. The chart that accompanies this chapter will give you a rough idea of how the various clubs differ in results. Remember, too, that the speed of the green is a big factor in your decision. A lofted 8-iron might work better than a 5-iron on an extremely fast green. You will have to learn by experience.

The important part of the chip-and-run shot lies in your ability to visualize the entire shot sequence before you swing. You should see in your mind's eye the one-third pitch and the two-thirds run and see the ball accomplishing those distances. It is most important that you locate a spot on the green where you want the ball to land before it starts its run. Once you have chosen that general area you must not waver in your decision. Right or wrong, make the stroke as you see it must be made. If your result is a shot short of the hole you can correct your judgment on the next similar chip.

I recommend that you always chip with one club number higher (an 8-iron instead of a 7-iron, for instance) if there is any doubt in your mind that your original choice of club will get your ball onto the green and onto the spot you have chosen. Then you will know that you have enough loft and will not worry that it will fall short onto the fringe of the green and be unexpectedly "killed" there, short of the hole.

Here is another good tip for successful executions of the chip-and-run shot: go down on the shaft of your club, even if it means going down as far as the steel shaft itself. The shortened shaft will give you greater control, especially on those little delicate shots around the green which require great touch.

Chip Shot Technique

Keep your weight entirely on your left side when you play the chip-and-run. The stroke is really nothing more than a lofted putt. There is a great similarity between the stroke on a long putt and the stroke of a chip shot. Play the ball back toward the center of an open stance with your hands ahead of the ball. Strike the ball with a descending blow, hands and wrists firm through the shot. The loft of the club does the work.

The chip shot is really a miniature swing, the only difference is that the body position at address is changed. The centerline of the body should run downward from the center of your head to a point left of the ball. The hands, too, are ahead of the ball. Since the ball stays in the center of your stance the set-up encourages a descending blow on the ball. The feet are closer together than they are on a full shot. The left foot is drawn back from the line so as to open the body more toward the target. This address position encourages the descending blow and helps to keep the ball on line toward the target. With the ball played back in the stance and the hands forward there is a better chance to strike the ball first, not the turf, on the downswing. Let the club do the work of getting the ball up and on its way to the hole.

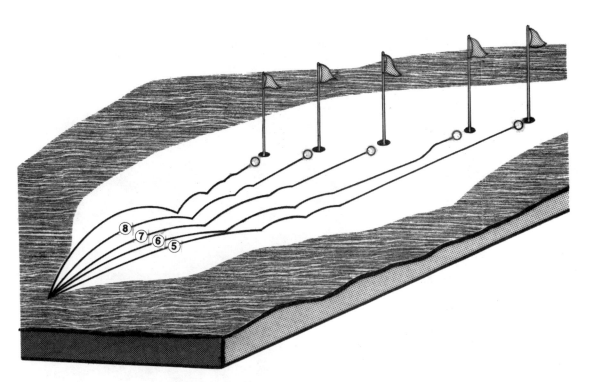

Here's a diagram illustrating the choice of club for a chip shot. The decision depends upon the distance the hole is from the edge of the green and also the distance between the ball and the edge of the green.

Here is a chip shot with the 8-iron. Notice that I have narrowed my stance to the point that my feet are almost touching each other. I have gone down to the very bottom of my grip for greater control. My weight is entirely on my left side. This stroke is like a long putt with the shoulders and arms taking the club back low to the ground and then through the ball with acceleration. The ball is struck a descending blow, a crisp hit which hits the ball first, not the turf.

Here's that same shot. The clubhead necessarily rises farther off the ground than it would in a long putt. That's so I can strike a descending blow on the ball. My head and body remain absolutely still. The only movement is in my arms and shoulders as they take the clubhead back and then down to accomplish this crisp hit.

Another sequence photo of the chip shot. I try not to hurry this shot at any time. Hurrying the downswing will change the rhythm of the shot and cause a fat hit. I let the club do the work of popping the ball onto the green so as to land on the pre-selected spot from which I expect it to run to the hole.

Here is a side view of the chip shot with an 8-iron. Notice that I have opened my stance by drawing my left foot away from the line. My upper body, however, remains square to the line. My weight is solidly on my left side. My grip is shortened to the bottom of the leather. I am thinking, "head still, let the club do the work."

The ball has been struck a descending blow. My body remains still, my head has not moved, my eyes are still looking at the point of impact. I will listen for the sound of the ball landing on the green before I allow myself to see the result of the shot.

The chip shot is executed with a crisp downward hit allowing the loft of the club to project the ball toward the hole. Notice how low the clubhead is in the follow-through here. There should be no feeling of lifting the ball. Let the club do the work.

When the pitching wedge is used for a chip shot the follow-through is a little higher than that with an 8-iron or 9-iron. You need not think about it—it happens automatically.

Here is a view of my follow-through on a lofted chip. My head has remained steady over the ball as I allow the club to swing freely, even lasting through the shot. These shots must not be hurried. I try to swing with constantly repeating smoothness and rhythm and let the club loft propel the ball where I want it to go.

I have put the white circle on the surface of the green to illustrate my mental approach to the shot. I see in my mind's eye the exact spot on which I must land the ball in order to have it run successfully to the hole. I suggest that you try this visualization trick. It works for me; I think it will work for you.

Here is a picture of my backswing on the shot. Notice that I have not broken my wrists and that I have taken the club away from the ball in one piece—that is, my arms, hands, and shoulders are all moving at the same time. I think of this shot as nothing more than a lofted putt because the ball will act like a putt once it has landed on the green. That is another reason for taking into account the slope of the green in determining where to let the ball land.

Here is a more lofted chip. My target area is a few feet farther onto the green than it was in the photo on page 50. I am using a pitching wedge here because there is a small rise in the green in the first few feet of travel toward the hole. My wedge will take the ball over that possibly troublesome area and land it softly where it can drift down to the hole.

I have laid the clubface of my 8-iron open, turning it into a 9-iron in effect. I want to see if I can duplicate the shot that I would make with my 9-iron. By switching clubs this way it is possible to achieve great control with both clubs. I recommend this practice.

I am trying to decide whether to chip this shot or putt it from the fringe of the green. If the shot is a long one, more than 30 yards, I will probably chip it. Shorter than that, I'll putt it. I recommend that you determine your own outer limit on the long putt, too. If you have trouble getting long putts close to the hole, the answer may be more practice in chipping the 30-to-50-yard distance to achieve more consistently successful results.

This ball is on the very edge of the fringe of the green. Although there is little resistance to be expected from the fringe itself, the grass behind the ball creates a problem. If my putter catches up in the grass the shot will be missed. I decide to use my sand wedge as a putter. I raise the blade so that it will strike the ball at its equator. The weight of the sand wedge overcomes the resistance of the grass behind the ball. This shot must be practiced a great deal to achieve proficiency.

Here I am chipping with my pitching wedge because a lower-numbered club would cause the ball to run beyond the hole. When you practice this shot try two or three different clubs in succession. Let each club land the ball on the same target spot and observe the results. You will eventually choose the right club for the chip instinctively.

I am always thinking of holing out. On this practice shot I am trying to make the ball go into the cup on the fly. This is great practice to train you to hit your target and will give you confidence to help you to get the ball up to the cup every time.

Here is the result of that shot. This photograph was taken at the instant the ball landed near the cup; but it did not go in. Later in the practice session I was able to hole one of these chips, however. That's the real thrill of golf, the whole purpose of playing: get that ball into the hole!

Here is one of the shots most golfers love to play because nearly every time it will come off successfully. The ball is lying in fluffy rough with lots of space for me to slip my club underneath it. I go down on the shaft a short way for better control. I keep my head still and use a lazy swing with a full follow-through. Sometimes I don't even look at the ball on a shot like this. I look at the spot behind the ball where the club will enter the grass on the downswing. I recommend that you wait until you hear the ball land on the green before you lift your head to see what has happened.

Here is a chip shot from a touchy lie. The ball is on short-cropped grass without much room for error—there is very little grass under the ball. The shot must be struck precisely without any bounce of the club beforehand. I lay the clubface open and play the ball forward in my stance. The swing is longer than you might think it would be, but it is slow and lazy with my head staying absolutely still over the shot. Hurrying the shot will frequently cause a miss. I let the loft of the club do the work.

Notice how intently I am watching the ball at the top of my backswing and how my head has remained absolutely still over the ball. On a shot like this I try to keep my eye on the back center of the ball and try to see the clubhead strike it. That way, I stay down and have no tendency to look up prematurely and spoil the shot.

Here is a shot from a difficult downhill lie. I must carry the bunker in front of me. That means I must get the ball up quickly. I use my pitching wedge but because I must strike down on the ball the loft of the club becomes that of an 8-iron or 9-iron. The ball will run more than normal on a shot like this, so if the flagstick is close forget about getting the ball near the hole. I keep my weight on my left side and keep my body very still. This is primarily a hands-and-arm shot.

Sometimes I find it necessary to go so far down on the clubshaft that my grip is actually on the steel. Here you can see that I have achieved a fairly level stance by bending my left knee as much as I can and by gripping the club on the steel. Since I will not have the usual power in my clubhead as a result of the shortened grip, I must plan to strike the ball a little harder than I would normally. This shot will have increased loft, too, so I'll compensate for that by pretending that my 9-iron is really an 8-iron. That's a good way to force yourself to hit the ball a little farther.

Here's another view. Notice particularly that I have established a firm foundation for this swing by putting my right foot deep into the sand. I must not move on this shot. A solid foundation is the most important part of executing this shot successfully.

When you are faced with a sidehill lie with the ball higher than your feet, the most important thing to consider is how you are going to keep your balance in the swing. Gravity will be exerting a pull on your body, trying to take you away from the ball back toward your heels. So the first thing is to find as comfortable a stance as possible and get your weight onto your heels. If the weight is there to start with, there will be no possibility of a shift from the toes to the heels. The stance should be more upright than usual with the knees flexed less than usual.

Since the ball will be closer, you must choke down on your grip. The face of your club will be closed at impact and this will direct the ball more to your left than you would expect in a normal flat lie. You must compensate for this tendency to hit the ball to the left by aiming a substantial distance to the right of the target. A sand wedge will pull the ball farther to the left than a 7-iron or 8-iron. You must learn the amount of correction through experience. Most golfers, myself included, do not allow enough correcting to the right to compensate for the pull.

Make a slow, short backswing, keeping your normal rhythm in the stroke. Do not try to overpower the shot by hitting harder than usual. It is better to take one club stronger—an 8-iron instead of a 9-iron, for instance—if you have any recurring problem making the shot. Remember that you will be losing distance because of the shorter swing and because you have choked down on your grip.

Think balance, steady head, slow backswing, good rhythm and you'll succeed. You will find great satisfaction in solving the problem of how much correction you need to make aiming to the right of your true target and pulling the ball on the line straight for the flagstick. It is even better when you hole out on a shot like this. You can do it. I've done it many times.

Here is a mean lie, but fortunately, one that is rarely encountered. The ball is almost at knee height in the grass and I must stand in the sand to make my swing. I have shortened my grip, going down so far my hands are on the steel shaft. Since the ball is so high the "pull effect" will be substantial. By that I mean that the clubface will be closed at impact and project the ball to the left. I compensate by aiming well to the right of the flagstick. Once again, my prime thought is "steady, unmoving head and body."

Here is another view. Notice that my feet are not down in the sand very deeply and that my balance is back on my heels. This improper balance will cause me to pull the ball to the left or even cause me to mis-hit the shot completely. You are permitted to have a workable stance so take advantage of the rules by digging your feet into the sand until they are level.

This shot is practically the reverse of the preceding one, in which my feet were below the ball. Widen your stance for better balance. Again choke down on the club for better control. Play the ball in the center of your stance. Since you will be striking down on the ball you will be decreasing the loft of your blade and the ball will come out lower than usual. Open your clubface and let the club do the work. Don't try to lift the shot. Go right down with it on the same plane as the slope of the hill. Your finish will be low and expect the ball to run.

3
THE BUNKER SHOT

The sand iron or sand wedge, as it is called today, is a lofted broad-soled club used to extricate the ball from sand. It is also used for pitching from heavy places or when the player wants to get the ball up quickly. The development of the sand iron has revolutionized bunker play.

The Encyclopedia of Golf

The bunker shot is a true oddity in the game of golf in that you do not strike the ball in making the shot. You slide the clubhead under the ball by hitting anywhere from an inch to as much as two inches behind the ball and forcing the sand to "explode" or "blast" the ball out of the bunker. The amount of sand cushion will depend upon the density and weight of the sand. This shot is considerably different in technique from the ordinary pitch shot because you do not allow the toe of the club to catch up to the heel as the clubhead enters the sand. The deep flange on the club's leading edge helps the club to slice under the ball and "pop" it out onto the green. You do not allow the clubface to close as it cuts through the sand. (But on a long bunker shot the clubface will close in order to make the ball carry farther than normal.) The ball should be played forward in the stance about halfway between the center of the stance and a line off the left foot. The swing is on an outside-in line to facilitate the cutting action of the blade. Keep your weight evenly distributed between both feet. Try to hit the sand the same distance behind the ball every time without variation. Control the length of the shot by the power of the swing. Think of pulling the heel of the club through the shot ahead of the toe and don't be afraid to hit with force. The bunker shot is missed usually because the golfer quits at impact.

Here is a long fairway bunker shot to a green 75 yards away. The ball is sitting up well and it looks like I can catch it with the clubface without striking any sand and lessening the power of the shot. I will use my pitching wedge on this shot because of its thinner flange.

Here is the start of my takeaway on this fairway bunker shot. I have dug my feet in solidly to assure me a good platform. My weight will stay entirely on my left side because I want to hit down on this ball and catch it cleanly.

Here is my backswing on the long fairway bunker shot. My hands are now at shoulder height. My head has remained absolutely still over the ball. I am concentrating on the back of the ball. My shoulder has turned well under my chin, showing that I have a good windup with my body.

Another view of the fairway bunker shot swing at shoulder height. Notice how far down my feet are in the sand. This three-quarter backswing with a full wrist cock gives me power. Sometimes you can find a second, more solid, layer of sand lying beneath the softer sand on the top. When you dig in deep this way you lower your swing arc by about an inch. To compensate for this I have gone down an inch on my club shaft.

Here is my completed follow-through on that shot with my weight well on my left side and the club and hands high. You should not be afraid of this shot. Moving the ball back in your stance will help you to catch it before you strike the sand.

Another view of the start of my backswing on the fairway bunker shot. Notice that the stance is slightly open. My hands and wrists are still in one piece, not having broken yet. My wrist cock will occur at shoulder height. That encourages a full body turn.

This is another view of the club in the backswing as it reaches shoulder height with the wrists beginning to cock and carry the club to the three-quarter position. Notice that the line of the club shaft and clubface point straight at the target—the flagstick on the green. This is an ideal hand and wrist position.

Another view of the three-quarter swing I employ on this 75-yard fairway bunker shot. Notice that I appear to be sitting down to the shot. My legs are flexed, my weight solidly on my left side.

A fraction of a second after I have made my swing. The sand that you see flying was taken after the clubface struck the ball. I am remaining "down" in the shot, an indication that I was able to strike the ball before the sand. The follow-through is not yet completed.

This ball is down in the sand in what I call a half-buried lie. In order to get it out I will close the face of my sand wedge more than I would for a normal sand shot. I will be sure to hit through this shot with more power than I would use if the ball were lying cleanly on top of the sand. A ball out of a lie like this one will run more than normal, so I will allow for that in my calculation of my distance to the flagstick.

A clean lie in a fairway bunker 75 yards from the green. The overhanging lip may present a problem so I open the clubface of my pitching wedge and plan to clip the ball out cleanly without catching any sand between the clubface and the ball on my downswing. Notice that the ball is played back in the middle of my stance to help me catch it cleanly.

Here the ball is lying well on a slight upslope in the bunker. I dig my left foot in deeper than my right in order to make my stance as level as I can. I cannot overemphasize the importance of balance on this type of shot as well as on any similar shot where the feet are not level with each other.

The backswing on this bunker shot is a little on the outside with my blade open so I can slice under the ball and pop it up quickly onto the edge of the green. I call this my "pop shot" because I feel the ball pops out of the sand in a nice high trajectory and sits down softly on the green. My follow-through is a full one.

The finish of that shot in the last two photos. The ball has come out nice and high and will stop quickly on the green with a lot of backspin. Notice that I have kept my balance and made a full follow-through.

Here is a horrible situation for any golfer and yet one must make the best of it. The ball is completely buried beneath a heavy bunker lip. With an extremely strong wallop, most of the time I can cut through the sand, catch the ball, and drive it right up through the lip and out safely onto the green. It's absolutely necessary that I maintain my balance so I have dug my lower shoe well into the sand. The swing is shorter than normal. The head must remain steady. Sometimes I'm lucky to move the ball just a few inches in a situation like this, but the ball will come out—most of the time.

Here's another nasty lie, this time with the ball buried in the face of the bunker. The overhanging lip will be a hazard because the ball might be caught in it on the way out in a normal bunker-shot trajectory. Therefore I will take an outside-in swing with my clubface wide open to cut under the ball and try to pop it almost straight up in the air.

Another view of the stance for a lie buried under the lip of a bunker. The most important problem is keeping my balance. With my left foot up on the bank, my right foot well dug in, I have a good chance to stay on balance and make the shot. In this type of shot be satisfied with getting the ball out of the sand.

Here's the "moment of truth" in the buried-lie shot. I have been able to keep my balance and have delivered a strong smash into the sand a couple of inches behind the ball. You can see the ball on its way out successfully. My head has not moved, showing I have stayed down with the shot, an absolute necessity in this situation.

Here's the full finish of that buried-lie shot. You wouldn't believe me if I told you the ball rolled into the hole! I have finally lost my balance but not until well after completion of the follow-through.

The Downhill Bunker Shot

Sometimes your ball will roll through a bunker and end against the back edge in a place where it is almost impossible to get the clubhead down into the ball. When this happens don't be afraid to try this way of getting the ball out: Dig your shoes well into the sand and take as steady a stance as you can under the circumstances. Choke down on the grip quite a bit and open the clubface wide open. On your backswing you must break your wrists very sharply in order to get the clubhead past the lip of the trap. You will also take the club back well to the outside of the line to the hole. Try to make your right hand catch up with the left as you go through the ball. This hand action will produce a cutting and scooping action that should get the ball up quickly and perhaps even near the cup. This is a very difficult shot so don't be upset if you do not carry it off successfully. Even the pros make it only part of the time.

A very difficult shot with the ball in the near upslope of a bunker. I am trying to visualize the spot behind the ball where my clubface should enter the sand. I am concentrating on keeping my balance. I will pick this club up quickly on the backswing.

Another view of the downhill shot. I have drawn my left foot back and laid the face of my club open. Although my weight is on the left I try not to let gravity pull me farther left and down into the shot. I must stay steady on this shot—the least amount of sway will cause it to fail.

The swing has started with a quick break of my wrists. It is most important that there be no body sway on a shot like this. I call this a "chop" stroke because the clubhead chops down into the sand behind the ball, skims under it, and gets the ball out on a fairly low trajectory without much spin. Be glad to get out of a lie like this. Don't worry about getting close to the hole.

Here's another terrible lie to contemplate—downhill on the back slope of a bunker. This is the shot that Mark Hayes executed successfully on the last hole of the Tournament Players Championship in 1977 to win the title. It is almost an impossible shot but if you open your blade as far as you can and slice down behind the ball you may get the ball out successfully. Good balance and great concentration are important. Be satisfied to get the ball out and expect it to run because it will not have any "stop" on it.

The Delicate Blast from a Sand Bunker

Sometimes you will find yourself in a sand bunker next to the green with the flagstick positioned so near the trap—say, within 20 feet—that you cannot play a full, conventional shot. Here's how to play the shot: Address the ball with a wide-open stance—that is, with the left foot well drawn back from the line. Play the ball off your left foot with the blade of your sand wedge turned very open. When you turn the blade in this way you bring the heavy flange more into play and encourage the club to bounce off the sand instead of digging deeply into it. Begin your swing by taking the club back on the outside and on a fairly low plane. In other words, do not bring the club up as abruptly as you would normally do for the conventional explosion shot. On the downswing, hit the sand about an inch behind the ball and "skim" the ball out, taking very little sand underneath it. Keep your wrists firm on the follow-through. This kind of wrist action will give you greater control of the shot.

To determine how much power you should put into this shot, picture in your mind a chip shot about half again as long as the shot that faces you. A final word of advice: Don't move your head or your body. Keep as steady as you can. This is one of the most difficult shots a golfer ever faces. Movement will spoil it for sure.

I started the last round of the 1982 Masters Tournament leading the field. Severiano Ballesteros and Jerry Pate were three shots behind me and Dan Pohl was six strokes back. At the end of the first nine I was coasting along nicely, six shots ahead of everybody. Then I ran into trouble on the back nine. I took 4 on the 3-par 12th and Dan Pohl, playing ahead of me, birdied the 13th and the 16th to pull within two strokes of me.

The 16th hole is a very dangerous 190-yard 3-par with water on the left all the way from the tee to the green. Trying to guard against going into the water, I overcompensated and put my tee shot into the bunker on the right, hole-high with the flagstick. I really had a frightening shot confronting me then. An ounce too much power might send the ball across the green and into the water hazard. I had to play a delicate blast, if a blast can ever be called delicate. I popped the ball out and it landed on the fringe only inches beyond the front edge of the bunker. The ball ran slowly down the slope in a perfect line for the hole. I thought it might go in. It did not, though; it touched the right rim of the cup without hitting the flagstick. If it had hit the stick I'm sure it would have holed. Then it started to roll down the slope. It finally stopped forty feet away from the cup. I couldn't believe my eyes. Nearly a hole-out and yet there I was, forty feet away. I did not make the putt. Pohl caught me at the 18th hole but I was fortunate enough to win in the playoff. You can be sure that I'll never forget that "delicate blast" at the 16th hole of Augusta National.

4
THE PUTT

The part of golf which takes place mainly on the putting green in which the ball is not made to fly but is rolled toward the hole with the purpose of "holing out" or leaving the ball near enough to the hole to accomplish this on the next stroke.

The Encyclopedia of Golf

My putting style is known as the "arm and shoulder" method. When I first played golf I used an arm and wrist method that worked well at times and then again would fail me, especially in clutch situations. You may remember that I played on the Walker Cup team in 1975. One of my teammates was Gary Koch, an extremely good putter who used the arm and shoulder method. Gary has gone on to become very successful in professional golf. We have played together many times. It finally dawned on me that Gary was a much better putter than I and that the reason for his success lay in his method. In the arm and shoulder method the hands are kept quite still and the wrists do not break. The arms and shoulders move as a unit in a pendulum fashion, taking the club back in what is actually a miniature golf swing, and then letting the clubhead swing through the ball easily and yet with the necessary acceleration at impact to deliver a consistent, authoritative stroke.

I decided to change my style to the arm and shoulder method. I have never regretted the change; the fact that I led the PGA tour in putting in 1985 vindicated my decision.

Although I do not know of any scientific studies to support me, I would say that the trend, especially among professional golfers today, is to use the arm and shoulder method.

Putting is often said to be "the game within the game," a part of the golf swing that varies in a hundred different ways from golfer to golfer. Basically it is true that if the putter blade strikes the ball at a perfect right angle to a certain predesignated line the ball will travel down that line and find the cup—that is, hole out—and a successful putt has been executed. How that putter blade reaches the ball is another matter.

There are essentially three different putting styles. Since the early days of golf the most prevalent style has been a combined arm and wrist stroke. Robert T. "Bobby" Jones, Ben Hogan, Walter Hagen, Horton Smith, and many other great golfers used this method. Thousands of golfers continue to use it today. Sometimes the stroke incorporated an effort to keep the blade square to the line all through the stroke by the action of hooding—that is, turning the blade under in a counterclockwise fashion at the start of the backswing and then the reverse, clockwise, fashion in the forward swing. Needless to say, the method, while successful for many great golfers, has many pitfalls for the ordinary golfer.

Another basic style of putting is called the wrist stroke. In this method the golfer uses only his wrists, very little arm movement, to "pop" the ball into the cup. In fact, the stroke is often called the "pop stroke."

Billy Casper, a wonderful putter, is an excellent example of this style. However, ordinary golfers have not been able to adopt the wrist stroke with much success.

Here are what I believe to be the fundamentals of a good putting stroke:

First, that intangible quality—*confidence*. I believe that great putters are born, not made. Some great putters simply have better nerve and muscle control than ordinary men have. In spite of that, I also believe that a golfer who is not a "natural" putter can develop skills on the green that can make him a good putter. Confidence comes from the use of a sound method and many hours of intelligent practice.

Second, I believe that a good putter must have a vivid *imagination*. He must be able to visualize the line the ball will take, over slopes and hills and valleys on the green, on its way to the cup. In my opinion, a putter will never be great without this ability. Again, how does one develop that skill of imagination? By practice and by using every sense of the body, especially the eyes and the sense of balance that feeds up through the body from the soles of the feet as the golfer walks onto a green and prepares to make the putting stroke.

Next, let's talk about the implement that does the work—the putter. There are thousands of different putter designs, weights, and lengths. Some good putters prefer the blade type, claiming they can square the blade to the line better with that design. Others prefer the mallet type, the heel- and toe-weighted models, and many hybrid types of both kinds.

I recommend that you find a putter that suits you. It should be one that you just "know" will roll the ball into the hole for you. It will be the right length for you, will sole itself sweetly and smoothly behind the ball and just wait for you to use it. That sort of putter is the kind that will build your confidence.

Stick with the putter until it completely deserts you. Then, and only then, find a replacement. You can try lots of different putters, but in the long run I firmly believe that it is not the putter but the "puttee" at fault when the ball will not go into the hole the way you expect it to do.

The grip can be your normal grip, overlapping, interlocking, or any of the variations in which the overlapping grip is reversed to put the left forefinger over the little finger of the right hand or down the shaft the way Arnold Palmer does. My own idiosyncrasy is that I put my right forefinger down the side of the shaft. I have always done this and since I feel I putt well with that grip, I am not going to change my style.

The grip should be a delicate one, definitely not a tight squeeze on the shaft. I feel that my left hand is a little firmer on the shaft than my right hand. The right is relaxed and ready to feel the putt.

Both hands should be on the shaft with equal amounts of control. The two hands must work together as one single unit transmitting the power to the blade from the movement of the arms and shoulders.

Your eyes must be directly over the ball. If they are not a phenomenon called parallax becomes a factor in determining the correct line of the putt to the hole. Parallax, a term used in the science of optics, is "the apparent displacement of an object as seen from two different points not in a straight line with the object." When the eyes are over the ball on a straight line toward the hole they are better able to visualize the correct line from the ball to the cup.

The putting stance should be wide enough to give you a solid foundation for a miniature swing. The stance should be square to the intended line with the feet and shoulders paralleling the line the ball must take to the cup. Very few putts are on a dead level surface so the body and feet should be squared to the line that the ball must travel, whether it is to the right or left of the cup. There is an old golf expression that says, "all putts are level—it's just that the cup is not where it is supposed to be." Many golfers make the mistake of lining up toward the cup and then pushing or pulling the ball to get it on the proper line. The weight is nearly all on the left foot and left side of the body; it should stay there throughout the stroke. The ball should be consistently played off a line running outward from the inside of the left shoe. This allows the clubhead to catch the ball on a slight upswing which imparts overspin to the ball and helps it to track steadily and surely to the cup.

The stroke is a rhythmic swing back and forth like a pendulum. The backstroke should be approximately as long as the forward stroke. The length of the backward and forward strokes is determined by the distance the ball must be struck.

The stroke must be smooth and unhurried. If possible, the golfer should concentrate on making as smooth a stroke as possible without caring (though, of course, he really does care) whether the putt is holed.

Most golfers use a slight forward press—a slight break of the wrists forward—before starting the putter back from the ball. This move is a natural one and helps to keep the putter blade on the inside of the line, a desirable feature of a good putting stroke.

I cannot overemphasize the importance of a steady, unmoving body platform. The slightest sway will cause the putter to lose its direction and the putt will be missed, either pulled left or pushed right.

The head and entire body must remain steady and stable to give a consistent, solid platform for the stroke which will be carried out by the arms and shoulders as they move backward and forward transmitting power through the hands to the clubhead so it can stroke the ball down the pre-selected line to the hole. By "steady and unmoving" I do not mean that the body should be stiff or tensed unnaturally. The body should be in a relaxed yet firm state. All good putters exhibit this quality of steadiness over the putt and continue to remain unmoving until the stroke has been made.

If you will carry out the sensible practice routines that I

recommend in this chapter, you will inevitably become a good putter. You may even become a great putter.

Let's review the basic fundamentals of a good putting stroke:

- Confidence, which is developed through intelligent practice and golf experience.
- An excellent imagination, also developed through practice and experience.
- A favorite putter that suits your putting style.
- A sound grip with hands in equal control of the stroke.
- Eyes directly over the ball.
- A square stance with the ball played off a line drawn outward from the inside of the left shoe.
- A balanced rhythmic stroke using the arms and shoulders to move the club in a pendulum fashion.
- A steady, unmoving body platform.
- Practice, practice, and more practice.

Now let's analyze some putting situations that actually occur on the golf course:

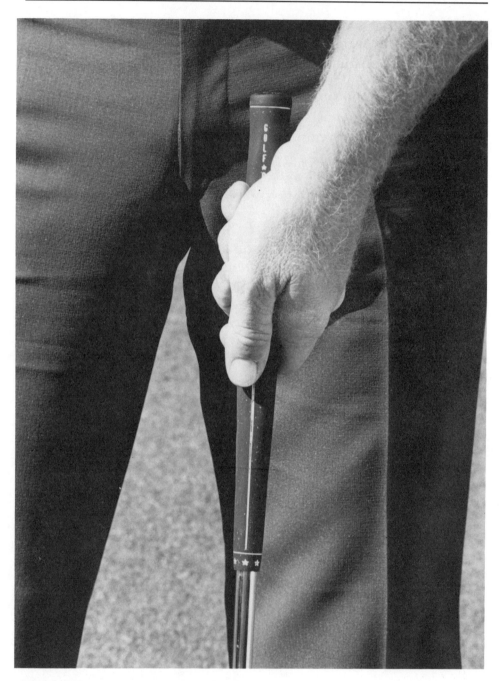

First, I put my left hand on the shaft.
My thumb is squarely on top, pointing
straight at the ball. I have the feeling
that the bones of my left hand are
facing my line at a 90-degree angle.

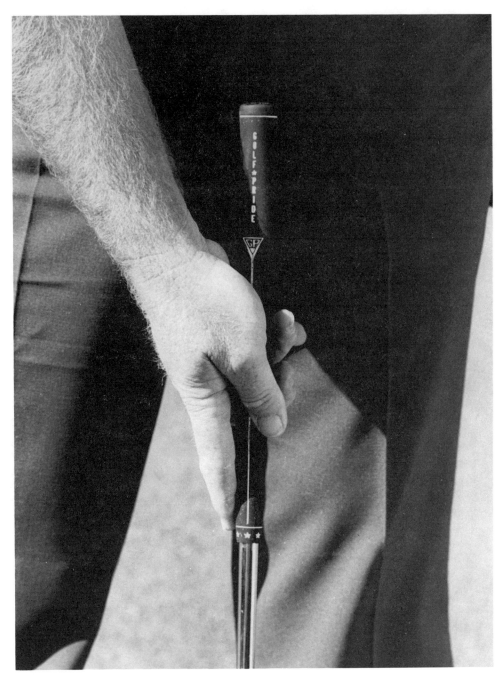

This is the way my right hand goes
onto the shaft (my left hand has been
removed for the sake of illustration). I
have the feeling that the palm of my
hand is at an exact right angle to my
intended line. My extended forefinger
is a personal idiosyncrasy. I like to
think of it as my "feeler."

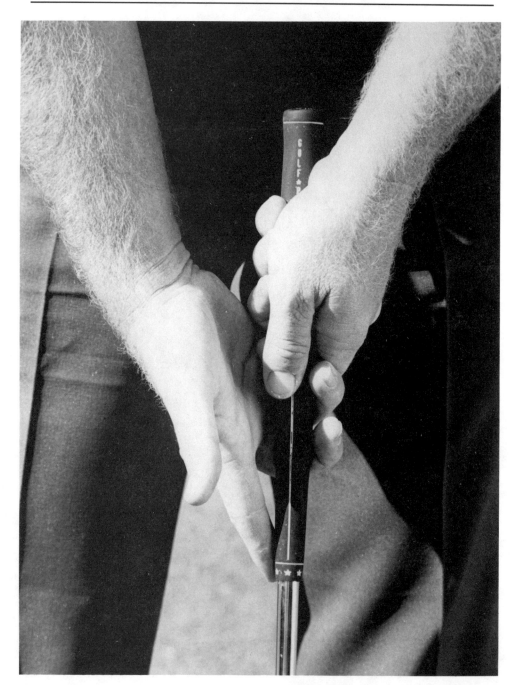

This is the way I assemble my putting grip. I put the tip of my forefinger down the shaft to the very end. I am visualizing my intended line and try to put it precisely at a 90-degree angle to that line. The thought is not unlike imagining a carpenter's square with one angle pointing at the hole and the other being the line up my shaft and through the palms of my hands.

Here is my putting stance completely assembled. The ball is played off a line running outward from my left foot. Most of my weight is on my left side. The club is straight down to the ball with my hands neither in front of nor behind it. The club is placed carefully behind the ball so that I can strike it in the center of the blade.

Another view of my putting stance. Notice that I grip my putter shaft about an inch down from the tip. I do this consistently because I like the balance of my putter with a slightly shortened grip. You may want to do this, too. The important thing is no matter where you grip it you must do it the same way every time.

The Long Putt

The long putt is one of the most difficult shots in golf. Every golfer fears the three-putt green and, of course, the farther away the first putt is from the hole, the greater is the likelihood of taking more than two putts to get down.

It is most important that the distance be gauged as accurately as possible. I walk toward the cup on a line parallel to my line, counting my paces as I go along. I stop a couple of steps short of the hole so that I don't disturb the surface of the green with my spikes. But I register in my mind that this particular putt is, for example, a 23-yard putt and how hard I must hit this putt to reach the cup. As I pace the green, I am sensing the slope of the green—down, up, sidehill—with the soles of my feet. My eyes are looking for shiny places on the green which will tell me that the green may be faster than normal. I pay special attention to the grass around the cup to see if the cup lies on a slant. If it does, it tells me that one side of the cup is higher than the other and that the ball dying at the hole will be more likely to come in on the high side.

Once my distance is established I try to see the line to the cup. In my mind's eye I envision a black line running from my ball to the cup. I picture my ball traveling along that line and I see it going into the hole. I plan to hole every putt (and every chip, too, for that matter).

If there is a sidehill break I move the cup in my mind's eye the necessary distance to the right or left and visualize the putt as a straight one. The break in the green will cause the ball to move to the right or left and allow the ball to hole out.

A long putt must be hit solidly. Most long putts that miss holing or coming close to the hole fail because they are not struck hard enough, or solidly, in the center of the putter. A putt miss-hit on the toe or heel of the blade will lose about 10 percent of its potential speed. So a 60-foot putt miss-hit may leave the golfer an uncomfortable six feet short of the hole, for a probably potential three-putt.

Some good putters advise picturing a six-foot circle around the hole and attempting to place the ball inside that circle. I try to hole the long putt every time and have found that if I try to do so I am inevitably within the six-foot circle, anyway. There are exceptions to this rule, of course, and we will discuss them when we talk about the "lag" putt, and putting for safety.

The backswing in a long putt in the 40-to-60-foot range. The swing is free and considerably longer than it would be for medium-distance putts. Notice that the clubhead is only slightly above the surface of the green. It is best to keep the blade low all the time, even on long putts. I am concentrating on accelerating through the ball and making sure I stroke the ball on the sweet spot of the face of my putter.

The stroke on a long putt, one of 30 feet or more, is a little longer than it is for putts at a shorter distance from 30 feet to 15 feet from the cup. I let the club swing freely through the ball and keep my head as still as possible until the ball is well on its way. My primary concern is to strike the ball on the sweet spot of my putter blade so that I don't lose any distance with the stroke.

A view of my backswing on a putt in the middle range, from 20 to 30 feet. Notice how low the blade is, barely of the ground. My hands and wrists are unbroken as the arm and shoulder movement have taken the club back about six inches. I am concentrating on the back of the ball and thinking "accelerate" through the stroke.

The Short Putt

Most short putts are missed because they are not hit firmly enough. The putt either dies before it reaches the cup or veers off because the speed of the ball decreases and allows the slope of the green or the grain of the grass to take too much effect.

Concentrate on making a firm stroke. Use a stroke that puts your putter blade through the ball, straight toward the hole. If you consistently putt aggressively, you will make more than your share of short putts.

The backswing on a putt in the three-to-five-foot range. Like the swing of a pendulum, the length of the backswing is the same as the length of the follow-through. There is a feeling of acceleration at the bottom of the arc. The acceleration comes from the clubhead weight without any action of the hands interrupting the rhythm of the swing.

Putting Survey

I am deciding whether to putt or chip the ball when it is lying just off the edge of the green. Here the ball is lying cleanly on very short grass. There should be little or no resistance from the longer grass so I will putt this ball rather than chip it. I will also take advantage of the fact that I can leave the flagstick in the hole since my ball lies off the putting surface. On a downhill putt it is often useful to let the flagstick act as a possible backstop should the ball strike the pole.

I like to start my survey from directly
behind the ball. I leave the flagstick in
the hole for a while to help me
confirm my estimation of the degree
of slope on the green. I squat down
because I feel I can see the line better
that way. I look for shine on the grass
which will tell me which way the grain
runs.

I am about to decide how hard I will stroke this putt and the line it will take to bring it in on the top side of the cup. I try to visualize a black line running from my ball right into the cup. I have now found a slight discoloration in the surface of the green about three feet ahead of the ball directly on my intended line. I will "spot putt" the ball over that mark. If I hit my mark I should have a good chance to hole the putt.

The easiest way to pace off your putting yardage is by walking alongside your intended line, starting at the ball and ending within a couple of paces from the cup. When you do this, there is another benefit: the soles of your shoes act as sensors and tell you about subtle slopes in the green.

Another way to pace off and count
the yardage of my putts. You should
do this on a line parallel to the line of
your putts so that you do not put any
spike marks in the line you intend to
take. Be careful, too, not to disturb the
line of other players' putts. I enter the
yardage in my total list of facts I need
to know before I make my stroke.

A look from the other side of the putt is useful, too. It helps to confirm my opinion about the degree of slope around the cup. It also confirms or changes my estimation of the way the grain of the grass will affect the putt.

Sometimes a small change in the viewing angle may bring to your attention an important fact you have missed from a low angle behind the cup. The glint of grain will vary from green to green and often depends upon sunlight to fully disclose the way it lies.

A survey from the side is useful
because it allows a good estimate of
the length of the putt. I like to look at
the putt from a point midway between
the ball and the hole. Sometimes I feel
as if I'm a civil engineer when I do this
but every factor that affects the putt
should be taken into consideration
before the stroke is made.

I have the flagstick removed from the cup. Now I try to visualize my putting line. On this green there is a slope to the right. In my mind's eye I see my ball tracking along a line a foot to the left of the cup and then, as it dies, taking the effect of the slope and falling into the left or top side of the cup. If my calculations are correct I will sink the putt. I try to imagine it going into the hole so I will have a positive thought before I make the stroke.

My mind is made up. I see the line and am confident that I know exactly how I will stroke this putt. I step into my stance with nothing but positive thoughts. I think "smoothness," "slow tempo," "acceleration through the ball," with acceleration as my final thought. With this survey routine, a smooth stroke, and a positive relaxed attitude I hole a great many putts.

At last I am completely prepared to putt. I step into a preliminary stance on a line a couple of inches away from my ball. I take two practice strokes emphasizing acceleration through the ball. Then I step forward, reassemble my stance, and without any further waste of time make the stroke.

The survey of a 20-foot putt. I can see that this cup is tilted from right to left. That tells me I must borrow a few inches from the right so as to bring the ball in on the top side of the cup. The putt is uphill, too, so I know I must stroke it a little bit harder. Since the putt is uphill I can be aggressive with my stroke because the ball probably will not roll very far past the cup.

Here is a putt on the same line from a distance of eight feet. I like to think of this putt as merely a long three-footer. My backswing will be shorter in length; the follow-through will be shorter, too. The effect of the right-to-left borrow will be less than it was on the 20-foot putt on the same line. Therefore, I can either putt boldly straight for the back of the cup or I might allow an inch or so on the left side if I want to let the ball die at the hole. A slowing ball will take the break more than a firm, aggressive, harder stroke. I decide on the bolder putt.

The Lag Putt

There are many occasions in golf when it is not wise to charge the cup—that is, to putt aggressively toward it. Most frequently this happens on extremely fast greens, particularly a downhill putt. It can happen, too, where the cup is on the edge of a plateau and you don't want the ball to slip past the hole and down the hill.

When I want to lag a putt I grip my putter very lightly and stroke the ball as delicately as I can, contacting it near the tip of the blade so that the full weight and power of the club are lessened. I also putt to an imaginary cup I see in my mind's eye a few feet short of the actual cup.

5
TROUBLE SHOTS

Every golfer gets into trouble some time in a round. It is important not to get upset. You must learn to accept your problem and figure the best and easiest way out. Have confidence in your swing. Practice as much playing out of bad lies as you practice out of good ones and you will never be afraid of a bad lie again.

Here are a few of the most common trouble shots golfers encounter along with my comments on how to deal with them.

One of the nastiest lies in golf—
against the far side of a divot hole.
This shot requires an aggressive
stroke. It is not unlike a punch shot
without much follow-through. I play
this shot back in my stance with my
hands forward to help me to hit down
on the ball.

Another view of the ball lying against the far side of a deep divot hole. While it is an unpleasant situation to have to face, it can be overcome with proper technique. I shorten my swing to make it more compact, close the clubface, keep my weight solidly on the left, and strike down on the back of the ball. Sometimes the ball comes out erratically when it is squeezed against the grass. That can't be anticipated or judged truly. Be happy to get out of such a bad lie.

Here the ball, while in a divot hole, is lying more favorably than it did in the preceding photo. The shot is much like a shot off the very hard ground, called hard pan. The ball must be struck first so it is played back in the stance, the hands forward, the clubface square or even slightly closed.

Here's the third type of "ball in a divot hole" lie you will encounter. This one is not as difficult as the other two. Once more I play the ball back in my stance, hands forward, and try to strike a descending blow. I will close my clubface, too. The ball will come out lower than normal and will have more run than usual.

A rear view of the divot hole shot in the preceding photo. My stance on this shot is square, my hands are ahead of the ball. I will concentrate on driving down through the ball and letting the loft of the club get the ball out successfully.

The top of the backswing as I dig this ball out of a divot hole. The swing is a little shorter than usual with the ball played back in the stance. The swing is a little steeper, too, to allow a descending blow which will pinch the ball out.

When your ball lies in deep rough, pretend you are in a bunker and pick out a spot a couple of inches behind the ball. That will be your aiming point. Concentrate on making a full swing with an exaggerated follow-through. Before I make a shot like this I like to visualize myself having completed a perfect follow-through and then I try to put the club in the position I saw in my mind's eye. If the follow-through is a good one it follows that the ball will have come out safely.

8-8

Here the ball is perched up high on deep rough. The danger here is that the club may slide under the ball too far and pop it up into the air. On this kind of a lie, shorten your grip to compensate for the raised position of the ball. Take a stronger club, too, because you will lose distance as a result of shortening your grip.

Pitch with the Ball in Deep Rough

When your ball is in the high rough your club must be swung hard enough to cut through a lot of deep, resistant grass before it reaches the ball, yet not so hard that the ball goes too far past the hole, or even over the green.

In this shot there will be increased torque from the grass trying to twist the club in your hands, so hold on to the club very firmly with your left hand. The right hand should also grip the club tightly, but not as strongly as the left. Keep the blade slightly open. Take the club straight up by breaking your wrists sharply at the start of your backswing. Use a slow, almost lazy swing. Take the clubhead all the way back and all the way through. Do not try to speed up your swing at any point. If you make this swing properly the way I tell you to do it, the ball will pop out of the rough cleanly every time, while the clubhead continues into the grass.

This shot can be played high or low. It is very effective in the 10-to-30-yard distance. Your lie in the grass and the placing of the flagstick on the green will determine how high you must hit the shot. For a high shot, you must play the ball more off the left foot, increasing the loft of the club. For a low shot, one that will run more after it lands, play it more off the right foot, decreasing the loft.

The Explosion Shot

The explosion shot is useful in many situations, besides being the shot of choice in a sand bunker. The explosion shot has saved me many strokes on shots I have made from wet turf, loose dirt, sandy rough, and pine needles. It is most effective when you are in one of these predicaments and are required to get the ball up quickly in order to clear some obstacle, such as water, a bunker, sand, bushes, a tree, or a mound. You should use either your pitching wedge or your sand wedge. Address the ball with the clubface wide open. Pick the club up rather abruptly toward the outside on the backswing and then come down about half an inch to an inch behind the ball. You must imagine that you are hitting the shot as if it were twice its actual length. You must be bold, making sure you follow through.

The shot needs a lot of practice, but if you master the shot even half the time your effort will be well rewarded.

In this trouble shot I must loft the ball quickly in order to carry a 50-foot pine tree in front of me. I lay the clubface open and play the ball far forward in my stance off the toe of my left foot. Another correction I will make is keeping my weight back on my right side. All of these factors put together will increase the loft of the club and will cause the ball to rise quietly and clear the obstructing tree.

Contemplating a clean sandy lie in the rough. The important thought here is that the ball must be struck without taking any sand behind it. Since it is not in a hazard I can ground my club behind the ball, an advantage I could not have if the ball were in a hazard.

I square my stance and grip down on the club. Since I am not in a hazard behind the ball, I play the ball well back in my stance, almost off my left foot. My hands are well ahead of the ball so I close the clubface to square it at impact. All of these adjustments help me to hit the ball cleanly and make a successful shot.

Putting Out of a Bunker

Putting out of a sand trap is a good percentage shot when all the conditions are right. First, the ball must be sitting up well on top of the sand. Second, the trap must be relatively flat and have no overhanging lip. It is also useful to have hard-surfaced sand like in a bunker that has not been raked recently. You can make the shot out of softer sand but your chances of muffing the shot are greater.

Address the ball with your regular putting grip and stance but make this change in your stroke: play the ball off the toe of your blade instead of in the center. Most putting strokes impart backspin to the ball; hitting it with the toe of the blade will help you to give a slinging action to the putt, will reduce the natural backspin, and increase the possibility of a more consistent roll. Use this stroke in an emergency—for example, when you might be afraid of a thin bunker shot that could take your ball over the green into water or another bunker.

Here is an example of a good opportunity to putt out of a bunker. There is water beyond the green and consequently the fear that a thin bunker shot might carry too far. The sand is hard packed and there is no lip on the trap. It is difficult to control the distance of this shot so use it only in an emergency, when you want to get out of the sand and don't care how close you get to the hole.

The Emergency Trouble Shot—Left-Handed

Once in a while you will find your ball near a tree or a fence and you will wish you were left-handed instead of right-handed. Don't be afraid to play the shot left-handed. Walter Hagen used to carry a left-handed iron for just such a problem; but these days when we are limited to no more than 14 clubs it is necessary to improvise a left-handed club. Take your 5-, 6-, or 7-iron and turn it upside down. Use a left-handed grip. You might grip the club as a back-handed right-hander or actually put your left hand in the lower position in the grip. Take a couple of practice swings emphasizing your steady head. You can make this shot if you don't try to get too fancy with it. Be satisfied with a clean hit on the ball and modest distance. This is a good shot to practice beforehand. If you've done it on the range you won't be too surprised when you have to do it on the course. If you use a blade putter rather than a mallet type you should always be aware of the possibility of reversing the club into a left-handed one. You would use it, obviously, where you are able to run the ball along the ground and not required to loft the shot to get out of trouble.

Rather than play the shot right-handed when you're too close to a tree, you can improvise a left-handed club.

Or you can reverse the club into a left-handed one.

For this shot, you can run the ball up to the flag.

The chop shot with the putter. Here's an effective way to get the ball out of moderately deep green-side rough. It can be used when you have no more than two or three feet between your ball and the cut surface of the green. Bring the putter up quickly in a steep backswing and chop down on the ball with good force. The ball will pop right out with considerable overspin. It's an unusual shot, but sometimes when you are afraid that a lofted club will be hard to control, the shot may work as well or better than a foozled wedge.

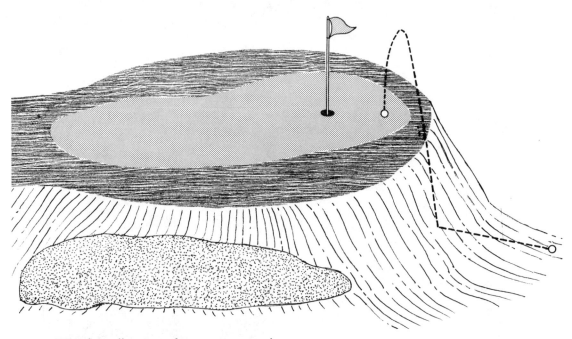

Here is a diagram of a most unusual trouble shot. It is called the "bump shot" because the ball is bumped into the steep slope of a green with considerable force and deflected upward. The ball will land very softly and quickly because the deflection angle drives it almost straight up into the air. It is a desperation shot and should be used only when the flagstick is so close to the edge of the green that any pitch would run by the hole a considerable distance. The conditions for the shot must be almost perfect for it to work successfully. The slope of the green must be very steep and the grass closely cut so that the ball will not catch up in it and lose its forward motion. Use a low-lofted club such as a 3-iron or 4-iron to drive the ball into the bank of the green. You will be surprised at the effectiveness of this shot. Find a slope like the one shown here and practice this shot. You will learn to recognize the slope angle necessary to make the shot work.

6
PRACTICING

I recommend that you devote no less than 25 percent of your practice time to putting.

Here's a good putting practice routine. Use five balls. Start first at a distance of no more than a foot from the hole and hole all the putts. That's to build your confidence in holing. Do that several times in a row.

Then move to a distance of 3 feet and begin holing the same five balls from the same spot. Aim for the center of the cup at first, and then for the edges, alternately right and left.

Then move to 6 feet, to 12 feet, and to 18 feet. Finally work at your longest putting distance, probably in the 50-to-60-foot range.

A routine like this should be used once a week. Of course, adapt it to your own putting ability. If you are weak on the short putts, work on them more than the others. I promise you that you will become a good putter if you carry out these instructions faithfully.

Long Putts

When you practice long putts, work at the longest putting distance you will customarily find on your home course. If your greens are unusually large, that might be a 40-to-50-yard distance. If they are smaller the distance might be in the 90-to-100-foot range. Try to find a range on your practice putting green that will let you putt back and forth between cups at your chosen distance. Try to work on an uphill putt going in one direction, a downhill putt when you come back.

I recommend that you use five balls in long-putting practice. If you have a putting partner, one will stay at one end of the range and the other player at the other end. The first player putts all five balls and the second one has to sink the second putts; and vice versa.

When you start putting the five second putts I suggest that you hole the putt that is closest to the hole first. It will be a confidence builder. Then take the next closest and so on until all second putts are holed or missed. Keep score by totalling the two-putts. You will be amazed at the way your long putting will improve if you do this practice once a week. Furthermore, putting with a partner or opponent is more fun than putting alone.

The Middle Distances

Twenty-to-thirty-foot putts are what I call middle-distance putts. Frequently they can be made. If you really work hard practicing putts of that length you will be surprised how many you will hole at that distance.

Select a suitable track in your practice putting green. Pace off the distance just as you would on the course itself in an official game. Register in your mind: "I have paced 10 steps from that cup so the distance is 30 feet." You might go on with your analysis somewhat like this: "This putt is slightly uphill; therefore, I must hit it harder than I would for a similar-level putt. I see a four-inch right-to-left. In my mind, I'll move the cup four inches to the right and see if I can hole it on the first try."

Then, from the same spot each time use the five balls and proceed to practice the 30-foot putt. You may hole the first effort; probably you will not. However, your first effort will confirm or not confirm your analysis of the amount of break and the power of your stroke for that distance. If the ball broke more than you expected, move your line and your imaginary cup farther to the right. If it broke less, correct your line and cup accordingly. If your distance is wrong, adjust that, too.

Continue putting at this distance until you have established your own personal performance record. If you hole one putt in

10 at first or even one putt in 20 you will have established a 30-foot "par" for yourself. It means that you should register in your mind that you should expect to hole one in 10 or one in 20 putts of similar length when you next play a full round.

As you work at this 30-foot range you will find yourself improving slowly but inevitably. Your odds on holing may go up to three, four, even five out of 20 attempts. The most important part of this practice is that you *will* improve your putting and, of course, your score will come down with every putt holed.

Although this idea is not original with me, I recommend it highly. Place five balls around a cup on a slope and attempt to hole them one after the other, moving in a clockwise direction; then repeat, moving counterclockwise. You will be amazed how this practice will pay off in holing short putts when you play a regulation round on your course.

Practicing the game of "bump." A ball is placed on the front edge in the center of the cup. The golfer tries to hit the target ball so precisely it falls straight into the cup. Hitting it on either side will force it to the right or left and indicate a less-than-perfect putt. This is an excellent practice method, one that makes the golfer aim at the center of the cup rather than the entire width of the cup.

A less-than-perfect practice putt. The target ball will be struck on the right side rather than dead in the center. This type of practice can be varied by alternately hitting the target ball on the right side, center, and left side. The purpose, of course, is to achieve great control of both putting line and distance. The stroke must be aggressive and accelerating in order to impart the energy necessary to hole the target ball.

A very good practice-putting device is to use a tee as your target. When you can hit the tee consistently you will also be able to hole a lot of putts as well. This practice can be developed further by placing a second tee some feet away and putting back and forth between them. Try to find a spot on the green which will give you a right-to-left break one way and a left-to-right the other way.

Here's another practice device which will help you to develop your aim. Take four tees and place them so that they narrow the approach to the hole. If you carry out this practice frequently you will find that you have put into your mind's eye the view of the narrow path into the center of the hole. When you putt for real you will see it in front of the holes on your golf course greens.

Here is one of the simplest yet most effective putting-practice devices. Put a white tee into the back of the cup a half-inch below the rim. Then try to drive the tee deeper into the ground. This practice develops an aggressive stroke and lets the golfer realize that he can hit a tiny target consistently. After a session of this practice, the hole will begin to look like a wash tub—a target that can't possibly be missed.

A close-up view of the target tee in the back of the cup for practice putting. This practice can be varied by placing one tee a half-inch to the right of the middle of the cup and another similarly located on the left. Then the golfer should "sweep" his practice putts, first to the tee on the left, then to the tee in the middle of the cup, then to the tee on the right. Consistent practice in this way will lead to great control and develop a delicate touch in putting.

The game of 1, 2, 3, 4. Place four tees at distances of two feet, three feet, four feet, and five feet from the cup. Starting with the closest tee attempt to hole all five balls in succession. Then move to the second tee, the third tee, the fourth tee; and then, in reverse, the third, the second, and the first. This is another method of gaining great control and putting touch. The game can be played against an opponent, keeping score of holed putts. It can also be adapted for practicing longer putts.

You can easily devise your own straight-line device. Any art supply shop can sell you a sheet of heavy art cardboard stock. Cut your own line to the hole and use it on short-putt practice. It will become so impressed upon your mind that you will see it in your mind's eye whenever you putt a short putt.

In this game of horseshoes Mary's two balls are closer to the hole than Julie's. Therefore, Mary has earned two points on her score.

Julie and Mary are practicing the 30-yard long putt. First, Julie putts downhill to the lower cup. Mary holes the second putts and then putts the balls back up the hill. After a few rounds, they reverse positions. This is an excellent way to learn how to gauge the speed and direction of long putts.

Mary putts all five balls uphill to
Julie, who holes the second putts and
then putts back downhill to Mary's
cup.

How to Practice Bunker Shots

I follow a set routine when I practice bunker shots. It has paid off for me and I recommend that you follow it, too. The purpose of organized bunker practice is to make you competent, even expert, in all kinds of bunker shots—easy ones and difficult ones, too.

Take about 20 balls into your practice bunker. First, practice your stroke without the golf ball: Draw a line in the sand with the sharp edge of the sole of your club. It should be about six feet long and extend outward on a line from your left shoe tip. Start at the nearest end of that line and work forward with practice swings. What you are attempting to do is standardize your sand shot swing, making it exactly the same way every time.

Try to strike the line in the sand in precisely the same place every time. As you work up the line you will see that one time your club is striking too far behind the line, another time too far in front. But soon you will begin to hit the line at the same place every time. You will also notice that although you are aiming for the line which represents a spot two inches behind an imaginary golf ball, the excavation of sand shows about a three-inch slash, not two inches. That is because the flange of the sand wedge trails the leading edge by an inch and enters the sand first. Don't worry about that—just try to take the same cut every time.

This practice will teach you two important things about your sand bunker play. First, it will accustom your mind to the fact that you do not look at the ball during the swing but instead look at a spot in the sand behind the ball. Secondly, it will standardize your swing so that when you do have the ball in front of you, your swing and the area of cut will be consistently the same.

After you have completed this practice put down about 10 golf balls in excellent lies in the sand. Using the same swing proceed to splash them out of the bunker. With the phantom ball practice behind you, you should be able to get them all out successfully.

Note the distance the ball travels after your standard shot. It might be 15 yards or it might be 25 yards. A great deal depends upon the weight and resistance of the sand in your particular bunker. Some sands are light and fluffy; others, like seaside sands, are heavy and require more power from the clubhead to deliver the same distance.

Continue your practice in the sand bunker by putting the ball in various different and more difficult lies. Put the ball in a downhill lie and an uphill lie and compare the different results you obtain.

To practice bunker shots of thirty yards or more it is necessary to swing harder, of course, and take a little less sand behind the ball; you must also close the blade of your clubhead as it enters the sand. The long bunker shot swing is more like that of a pitch of 50 yards or more with a complete release of the hands through the ball.

An excellent practice at the end of your session is to step on the ball and bury it halfway into the sand. Make a swing and get that one out by closing your blade and hitting a little harder than usual. For your next shot have a good lie with the ball sitting up nicely on top of the sand. Then, step on the next ball and get it out onto the green. This—what I call alternate practice shots—will work miracles in your bunker play. The result will be that you will not be afraid of any bunker lie you encounter. You know you can get the ball out of the bunker and with lots of diligent practice you will become a capable bunker player, possibly an expert one.

This is the infamous "fried egg" lie which golfers often encounter when the ball comes down into the sand from a high trajectory. It appears to be a more difficult shot than it really is. Close the face of your sand wedge, square your stance, and play it as if it is a shot out of a divot mark on the fairway. The ball will come out running, but it will come out. You should practice this shot frequently. Then when you must execute it you will not be afraid of it.

You do not have to wait for a
rainstorm to practice bunker shots out
of wet sand. Take a couple of buckets
of water and soak the sand in your
practice bunker. The water makes the
sand heavier, so you do not need to
take as much sand behind the ball as
you would normally in a dry lie. That
means your club will be entering the
sand closer to the ball, opening the
possibility of a thin hit. So be careful
to stay down on this shot. Close the
blade to square to the line and be sure
to follow through. The shot requires
more power than you would use in a
similar dry lie, so adjust your swing
accordingly by playing for a spot a
few feet beyond the flagstick.

Practice Away from the Golf Course

There are many opportunities in your daily life for mental and physical practice of the golf swing when you are nowhere near a golf course or golf practice facility.

I recommend that you use every chance you find to make mock golf swings. By a mock golf swing I mean putting your body into a golf stance and swinging your hands, arms, legs, and body in a complete but phantom swing—that is, with no golf club in hand.

Put a golf ball down on the floor in front of a full-length mirror. Assemble your grip and stance and make a mock swing at that target. If you place your body toward the extreme right edge of the mirror you will be able to easily see whether you are swaying on the shot. If your head moves to the right out of view, obviously you did not keep your head steady throughout the swing.

In making a mock swing you can concentrate on taking the imaginary club away in the same motion that you let your left shoulder and left knee move into the backswing. That is an excellent way to learn the one-piece takeaway which is so useful and necessary for an effective golf swing. Another excellent practice method in the privacy of your home or office involves the use of a shortened club with a weighted tip. There are many examples of such a practice device.

Using a short practice club is a good way to build up strength in your left hand, left wrist, and entire left side. Take the club back to shoulder height on your backswing. Then start it down with as much acceleration as you can summon. The move begins with your left heel coming down and the left knee moving to the left side of your body. Then as the club comes down in the mock swing you must attempt to stop the club at the point of impact. You will not be able to stop the club, but the effort to do so will result in strengthening your left wrist and arm and give you a very important foundation for a good golf swing.

When you ride an elevator alone you often have a minute or more with your thoughts and your golf swing. Take advantage of such an opportunity to practice your mock swing. Think rhythm and smoothness. Think of the golf swing as a beautifully timed dance step. Swing, swing, swing every chance you get all day, every day.

You can make your own practice targets easily with a few milk baskets from a nearby convenience store. Keep a count of your hole-outs and the shots that stop within five yards of the target. In that way you can determine your odds of getting close to the flagstick in a regular round of golf. Always walk off the distance to the target so you know the length of the shot you are practicing.

Mental Practice

Horton Smith, a great professional golfer of the 1930s, winner of the first and third Masters tournaments, was a strong advocate of mental practice of the golf swing. He claimed that he put himself to sleep at night by rerunning in his mind the putts he had holed that day and replaying the best shots of that round. He tried to recapture and freeze in his mind exactly how his body felt and what he was thinking when he made those good shots.

I recommend mental practice as an excellent way to condition your mind to approach each shot, each putt in a positive manner. By practicing a particular shot over and over you will find that you will establish a rhythm in your swing that eventually will put your mind and body on "automatic." Just as a pilot of a transcontinental airline is able to set an automatic pilot mechanism which keeps the plane on its proper course, you too can train your mind and body to react automatically and successfully to the golf shot that faces you.

That is why I recommend intensive practice of a particular shot or putt rather than practice at random. I don't mean that you should not practice with all of your clubs one after the other. Of course you should, but I believe that 75 percent of your practice should be with only one club in an effort to master that single club. That is why I recommend that you adopt the 8-iron as your chip-and-run club. You will most certainly find many situations in chipping where it will be necessary to use a club other than the 8-iron in order to get more or less loft at the start of the shot or more or less run at the end of the shot. When you have mastered that one club, whether it be your 7-iron, 8-iron, or 9-iron as your "chipper," you will have built a basis of confidence in that most important stroke. There is not a more hopeless feeling in golf than to look down at a thin lie and say to yourself, "There's no way I can make this shot." On the other hand, if you have practiced chipping hundreds of balls from thin lies you will have built a foundation of confidence in your ability to successfully chip out of a thin lie. And you will not have that negative thought as you prepare to swing the club—you will have a positive, confident thought instead.

Try the Horton Smith sleeping pill. Recall your best shots and successful putts of the round that day. The idea works for me and it may work for you, too.

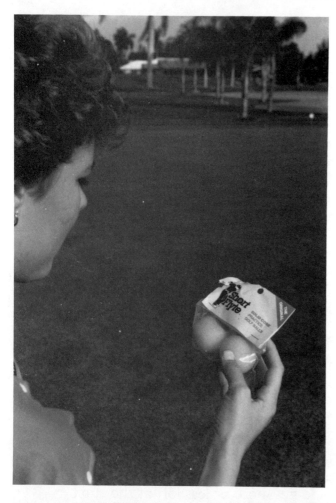

You have no excuse for not practicing your short game in your own backyard. The "Short Flyte" soft golf ball is a solid-core practice golf ball that flies only a few yards even when it is struck with the force of a full swing. The ball is available at golf supply shops and costs very little.

INDEX